How To Use This Study Guide

This five-lesson study guide corresponds to *"You Are the Salt of the Earth"* *With Rick Renner* (Renner TV). Each lesson in this study guide covers a topic that is addressed during the program series, with questions and references supplied to draw you deeper into your own private study of the Scriptures on this subject.

To derive the most benefit from this study guide, consider the following:

First, watch or listen to the program prior to working through the corresponding lesson in this guide. (Programs can also be viewed at **renner.org** by clicking on the Media/Archives links or on our Renner Ministries YouTube channel.)

Second, take the time to look up the scriptures included in each lesson. Prayerfully consider their application to your own life.

Third, use a journal or notebook to make note of your answers to each lesson's Study Questions and Practical Application challenges.

Fourth, invest specific time in prayer and in the Word of God to consult with the Holy Spirit. Write down the scriptures or insights He reveals to you.

Finally, take action! Whatever the Lord tells you to do according to His Word, do it.

For added insights on this subject, it is recommended that you obtain Rick Renner's book *Easter: The Rest of the Story*. You may also select from Rick's other available resources by placing your order at **renner.org** or by calling 1-800-742-5593.

TOPIC

You Are the Salt of the Earth

SCRIPTURES

1. **Matthew 5:13** — Ye are the salt of the earth: but if the salt have lost his savour, wherewith shall it be salted? it is thenceforth good for nothing, but to be cast out, and to be trodden under foot of men.

2. **Mark 9:50** — Salt is good: but if the salt have lost his saltness, wherewith will ye season it? Have salt in yourselves....

3. **Luke 14:34,35** — Salt is good: but if the salt have lost his savour, wherewith shall it be seasoned? It is neither fit for the land, nor yet for the dunghill; but men cast it out. He that hath ears to hear, let him hear.

GREEK WORDS

1. "salt" — **ἅλας** (*halas*): one of the most expensive and valuable commodities in the ancient world; the phrase "worth your salt" was a term used to describe a person's value; in the Roman military, soldiers were partially paid in salt, and it indicated a person was deserving of his salary or wages; salt was principally used seven ways — to depict what is valuable, as a preservative, as a flavor enhancer, as an antiseptic, as a medicinal and healing agent, to give protection from and to drive away evil spirits, and as a fertilizer

2. "savour" — **μωραίνω** (*moraino*): flat; foolish; tasteless; stupid; where we get the word moron

3. "good for nothing" — **ἰσχύω** (*ischuo*): literally, having lost its fullness; having lost its might; having lost its power; having lost its strength

4. "trodden" — **καταπατέω** (*katapateo*): to be walked on; to spurn; to treat with indignity

5. "under foot of men" — **ὑπὸ τῶν ἀνθρώπων** (*hupo ton anthropon*): under men; meaning under the feet of people

6. "good" — **καλός** (*kalos*): attractive; beneficial; wonderful; one of the most expensive and valuable commodities in the ancient world

A Note From Rick Renner

I am on a personal quest to see a "revival of the Bible" so people can establish their lives on a firm foundation that will stand strong and endure the test as end-time storm winds begin to intensify.

In order to experience a revival of the Bible in your personal life, it is important to take time each day to read, receive, and apply its truths to your life. James tells us that if we will continue in the perfect law of liberty — refusing to be forgetful hearers, but determined to be doers — we will be blessed in our ways. As you watch or listen to the programs in this series and work through this corresponding study guide, I trust you will search the Scriptures and allow the Holy Spirit to help you hear something new from God's Word that applies specifically to your life. I encourage you to be a doer of the Word He reveals to you. Whatever the cost, I assure you — it will be worth it.

> Thy words were found, and I did eat them;
> and thy word was unto me the joy and rejoicing of mine heart:
> for I am called by thy name, O Lord God of hosts.
> — Jeremiah 15:16

Your brother and friend in Jesus Christ,

Rick Renner

You Are the Salt of the Earth

Copyright © 2025 by Rick Renner
1814 W. Tacoma St.
Broken Arrow, OK 74012-1406

Published by Rick Renner Ministries
www.renner.org

ISBN 13: 978-1-6675-1146-7

ISBN 13 eBook: 978-1-6675-1147-4

7. "saltness" — ἄναλος (*analos*): bland; flat; insipid; tasteless; unsalty
8. "season" — ἀρτύω (*artuo*): to prepare; to adjust; to correct
9. "have" — ἔχω (*echo*): to have, to hold, and to possess
10. "fit" — εὔθετος (*euthetos*): fit; suitable; useful; literally, means it loses its place
11. "land" — γῆν (*gen*): here, referring to the soil
12. "dunghill" — κοπρία, (*kopria*): dunghill or manure
13. "men cast it out" — ἔξω βάλλουσιν αὐτό (*exo ballousin auto*): they are throwing it out; they are casting it away

SYNOPSIS

The five lessons in this study titled *You Are the Salt of the Earth* will focus on the following topics:

- You Are the Salt of the Earth
- Salt Was Very Valuable and Salt Was Used as a Preservative
- Salt Was Used as a Flavor Enhancer and Salt Was Used as an Antiseptic
- Salt Was Used as a Medicinal and Healing Agent and To Protect From and To Drive Away Evil Spirits
- Salt Was Used as Fertilizer

In Matthew 5:13, Jesus made this startling statement: "You are the salt of the earth." But what does it mean? Why compare us with salt? Although salt is abundant in our day, in New Testament times, salt was rare and quite valuable. Jesus knew this and so did the hearers of His message. In this series, we will unpack the deeper significance of Jesus' statement and discover some fascinating facets about salt and how they apply to us as believers.

The emphasis of this lesson:
Jesus has called His followers to be like salt in the world. This means we are very valuable and are to function as a preservative, a flavor enhancer, an antiseptic, a medicinal and healing agent, a fertilizer, and protection from and to drive away evil spirits. We're not supposed to be bland, tasteless, flat, or lifeless.

Seven Ways Salt Was Used in the Ancient World

During Jesus' famous sermon on the mount, He made this interesting and powerful statement: "Ye are the salt of the earth: but if the salt have lost his savour, wherewith shall it be salted? it is thenceforth good for nothing, but to be cast out, and to be trodden under foot of men" (Matthew 5:13).

Like everything Jesus said, each one of these words is packed with great meaning. The most important word here is "salt," which in Greek is the word *halas*. Salt was one of the most expensive and valuable commodities in the ancient world. Maybe you have heard the phrase "worth your salt." This was a saying used to describe a person's value. In the Roman world, soldiers were partially paid in salt, so when someone said, "That person is really worth his salt," it indicated he was very valuable and deserving of his salary or wages.

In ancient times, salt was principally used seven ways: 1) Salt depicted what was valuable. 2) It was used as a preservative. 3) It was used as a flavor enhancer. 4) Salt was used as an antiseptic. 5) It was used as a medicinal and healing agent. 6) People used salt to provide protection from and to drive away evil spirits. 7) Salt was used as a fertilizer.

How Does This Apply to Us?

So when Jesus said, "You are the salt of the earth," He was declaring many important things about us. First, He was stating that we are *valuable* to the world. Secondly, He was saying the presence of Christians and the Church as a whole should be *a preserving and restraining force* in the world. We are to preserve life and hold back corruption.

Third, the Church is to be *a flavor enhancer*, increasing the flavor of life for those around it. In other words, when Christians are being Christ-like and on-fire for Him, life should not be bland. Additionally, when we, the Church, are living the way we were meant to live, we are to be like *the antiseptic force* of God in the earth that drives out the bacterial-like effects of sin and the foul influences in the world.

The fifth use for salt was as a medicinal and healing agent. This means that we as believers are to be *medicinal* and bring the *healing* power of God to a world that is sick, diseased, and dying. Another use for salt was to drive away and provide protection from evil spirits. As believers, if we're really doing our job as the salt of the earth, we should bring freedom from foul, evil influences. The presence of Christ living in us and our standing against the enemy should drive out demonic spirits and provide protection so no evil can touch where we are.

Lastly, salt was used as a fertilizer, which means wherever we go, we are to be *a fertilizing influence*. Our lives ought to bring positive growth and productivity wherever we are on the earth. We should bring life to the people around us with our words and our actions.

All these meanings are packed into the word "salt"— the Greek word *halas*. When Jesus said, "You are the salt of the earth," these are all things He was declaring about us.

What Happens When the Church Is No Longer 'Salty'?

Immediately after Jesus said, "You are the salt of the earth," He went on to say, "…But if the salt have lost his savour, wherewith shall it be salted? it is thenceforth good for nothing, but to be cast out, and to be trodden under foot of men" (Matthew 5:13). There are several important words in the balance of this verse, so let's unpack them, beginning with the word "savour."

In Greek, "savour" is a form of the word *moraino*, and it describes *that which is flat, foolish, tasteless*, or *stupid*. It is where we get the word *moron*. By using this term, Jesus is telling us that when the Church is no longer providing its salt-like qualities, it loses its reputation. Suddenly, it becomes *bland, flat*, and *tasteless*, and in the eyes of the world, the Church is so *foolish* and *stupid* that no one wants to take part in it anymore. We as the Church need to be very careful about what we say and what we do because the world is watching us.

Again, Jesus said, "…But if the salt have lost his savour, wherewith shall it be salted? it is thenceforth good for nothing…" (Matthew 5:13). The phrase "good for nothing" is translated from a form of the Greek word *ischuo*, which literally means *having lost its fullness, having lost its might, having lost its power*, and *having lost its strength*.

Essentially, Jesus is saying, "When the Church begins to act moronic, how shall it be corrected? How can it regain its reputation once it's been lost? When the Church — or a believer — becomes tasteless, foolish, and stupid and it has lost its fullness, its might, and its power, it is good for nothing but to be cast out and to be trodden under the feet of men."

The word "trodden" in this verse is a form of the Greek word *katapateo*, which means *to be walked on*, *to spurn*, or *to treat with indignity*. When we, the Church, are no longer providing the salt-like qualities we are meant to provide, the people in the world walk all over us, spurning us and treating us with indignity. The phrase "under foot of men" — *hupo ton anthropon* in Greek — means *under men* or *under the feet of people*.

Mark's Gospel Reiterates Jesus' Call for Believers To Be Like 'Salt'

This principle of believers being the salt of the earth that Jesus presented is so important that the Holy Spirit moved Mark to record it in his gospel as well. In Mark 9:50, Jesus said, "Salt is good: but if the salt have lost his saltness, wherewith will ye season it? Have salt in yourselves...."

As in Matthew 5:13, Jesus compared believers to "salt" and used the same Greek word *halas*. Remember, salt was one of the most expensive and valuable commodities in the ancient world. In fact, the words "worth your salt" were used to describe a person's value because in the Roman world, soldiers were partially paid in salt. To say someone was "worth his salt" indicated he was deserving of his salary or wages.

Jesus chose the word "salt" because people were very familiar with it and were aware of its seven primary uses. In addition to depicting what is *valuable*, salt was used as a *preservative*, as a *flavor enhancer*, as an *antiseptic*, as a *medicinal and healing agent*, as a way *to give protection from and to drive away evil spirits*, and as a *fertilizer*. When Jesus said, "Salt is good," He was describing the Church and saying that as believers, we provide all the wonderful benefits of salt.

This brings us to the word "good," which is a form of the Greek word *kalos*, meaning *attractive*, *beneficial*, and *wonderful*. As Christians, when we are doing our job as the salt of the earth, we make Jesus and the Gospel *attractive*, we become *beneficial* to those around us, and we make our environment *wonderful*.

It Is Hard To Correct and Restore
a Compromised Reputation

In contrast, Jesus said, "…If the salt have lost his saltness, wherewith will ye season it?" (Mark 9:50). The word "saltness" in this verse is a form of the Greek word *analos*, and it describes *that which is bland, flat, insipid, tasteless, or unsalty*. We are to be so salty with God's goodness that it makes the people around us hungry for more of what we have. If we lose our saltiness, we become dull and tasteless to others.

When Jesus says, "…Wherewith will ye season it?" (Mark 9:50), the word "season" is a form of *artuo* — meaning *to prepare, to adjust*, or *to correct* — and its use here indicates that once a person has lost his "salty" reputation, it's very hard to correct and restore that reputation to him. This truth seems to have a connection to what Solomon wrote in Ecclesiastes 10:1, where he said, "Dead flies cause the ointment of the apothecary to send forth a stinking savour: so doth a little folly him that is in reputation for wisdom and honour." When a person who has a reputation for wisdom and for honor allows a little folly or foolishness into his life, that folly he permits gives him a *stinking reputation*, which can be quite difficult to fix once it's occurred.

Jesus wants us to be like salt and bring all its wonderful qualities to the world around us. We're not supposed to be bland, tasteless, flat, or lifeless. Instead, He commands us, "…Have salt in yourselves…" (Mark 9:50). The word "have" is a form of the Greek word *echo*, and it means *to have, hold, and possess*.

Therefore, when Jesus says, "Have salt in yourselves," it is the equivalent of Him saying, "You are supposed to be like good salt! You are *to have, hold, and possess* all the various good qualities of salt in your life."

Luke's Gospel Also Documents
Jesus' Charge To Be 'Salt-like'

Like Matthew and Mark, Luke also captured Jesus' comparison of the Church with salt. In Luke 14:34, he recorded Jesus as saying:

Salt is good: but if the salt have lost his savour, wherewith shall it be seasoned?

Once more we see the word "salt"— the Greek word *halas* — which was one of the most expensive and valuable commodities in the ancient world. Jesus said that salt is "good," again using a form of the Greek word *kalos*, describing *something attractive, beneficial*, or *wonderful*. When you as a believer are doing your job to be the salt of the earth, you make the Gospel more *attractive*, and people see you as a *benefit*. They will want you around because you help make the environment more *wonderful*.

At the same time, Jesus also said, "...But if the salt have lost his savour, wherewith shall it be seasoned?" (Luke 14:34.) The phrase "lost its savour" is a form of the Greek word *moraino*, the same word used in Matthew 5:13. It describes *something that is flat, foolish, tasteless*, or *stupid*, and it is where we get the word *moron*.

Jesus is clearly telling us that when we as Christians *lose our saltiness*, we become moronic — we do dumb, foolish things and become tasteless to the world. Considering this, Jesus asked, "...Wherewith shall it be *seasoned?*" (Luke 14:34.) In other words, how can the damage to our reputation be corrected and restored?

This is quite a sobering warning and lets us know we really need to be careful about what we do and what we say. The Bible says, "In the multitude of words sin is not lacking, but he who restrains his lips is wise" (Proverbs 10:19 *NKJV*). Never forget, a lost world is watching us. God desires us to have salt in ourselves and thereby be good, attractive, and beneficial to others.

Be Careful Not To Lose Your Place

Continuing with the analogy of the Church being like salt, Jesus went on to say in the very next verse:

> **It is neither fit for the land, nor yet for the dunghill; but men cast it out. He that hath ears to hear, let him hear.**
> **— Luke 14:35**

In this passage, the word "fit" is a form of the Greek word *euthetos*, and it means *to be fit, suitable*, or *useful*. In this verse it is used in a literal sense to mean *to lose one's place*. There are many Christians who used to be very powerful and effective, but they have lost their place because they lost their saltiness.

The fact of the matter is we have a great responsibility in being the salt of the earth. We must be very careful with what God has given us and not lose our place. There are churches, ministries, and individuals that have lost their place because of foolish words or stupid behavior. Jesus said that if we lose our saltiness and act moronic, we are "…neither fit for the land, nor yet for the dunghill…" (Luke 14:35).

The word "land" in Greek is the word *gen*, and it describes the *soil*. And the Greek word for "dunghill" is a form of *kopria*, which means *dung hill* or *manure pile*. Salt that has lost its qualities is no longer fit for the soil or for the manure pile. Instead, "…Men cast it out…" (Luke 14:35).

The phrase "men cast it out" in Greek literally means *they are throwing it out* or *they are casting it away*. Being thrown out or cast away is related to losing the place one previously had. There have been many people who were once powerful and were major influencers for God but lost their place because of foolish words or actions and their reputation became irreparable.

Although sometimes a loss of position is the result of legitimate demonic attacks, very often we ourselves open the door to these attacks by the foolish things we do. That is why Jesus is urging us to *have salt in ourselves* and be serious about who He has called us to be. He concluded by saying, "…He that hath ears to hear, let him hear" (Luke 14:35). We must open our spiritual ears to hear what God is speaking to our hearts so we continue to allow His salt to infiltrate and season our lives.

STUDY QUESTIONS

> Study to shew thyself approved unto God, a workman that needeth not to be ashamed, rightly dividing the word of truth.
> — 2 Timothy 2:15

1. Out of the seven primary purposes for salt and their application to us as believers, which one(s) stood out to you as most eye-opening and impactful? Why is that?
2. In Mark 16:17 and 18, Jesus said five specific things would take place for those who believe. Name these five supernatural signs we as believers can and should expect to be happening in our life as we stand on and believe in *the name of Jesus*.

3. In the book of Acts, we see the newly birthed Church actively being the "salt of the earth," just as Jesus said. According to Acts 2:42-47, what are some of the ways "salt-like" believers are to act?
What was the attitude of people *outside* the Church toward believers? (*See* Acts 5:11-13 and 2:47.)

PRACTICAL APPLICATION

But be ye doers of the word, and not hearers only,
deceiving your own selves.
— James 1:22

1. Ecclesiastes 10:1 says that when a person who has a reputation for wisdom and honor allows a little folly or foolishness into his or her life, it gives that person a stinking reputation. Take a moment to seek God and pray, "Lord, is there an area of my life where I'm allowing foolishness to enter? Have You tried to warn me about it, but I've ignored it? Please show me." Be still and listen. If the Holy Spirit shows you something, repent and ask for God's forgiveness. Then take the needed steps to make a clean break from that folly.

2. If the people you are closest to — at home, at work, and in your community — were to be asked if you exhibit "salt-like" qualities, how do you think they would answer? What attitudes and actions in your life might they point to that demonstrate the qualities of salt?

TOPIC

Salt Was Very Valuable and Salt Was Used as a Preservative

SCRIPTURES

1. **Matthew 5:13** — Ye are the salt of the earth....
2. **Mark 9:50** — Salt is good: but if the salt have lost his saltness, wherewith will ye season it? Have salt in yourselves....
3. **1 Peter 1:18** — Forasmuch as ye know that ye were not redeemed with corruptible things, as silver and gold, from your vain conversation received by tradition from your fathers.
4. **1 John 3:1** — Behold, what manner of love the Father hath bestowed upon us, that we should be called the sons of God....
5. **2 Corinthians 4:7** — But we have this treasure in earthen vessels, that the excellency of the power may be of God, and not of us.
6. **2 Thessalonians 2:3** — Let no man deceive you by any means: for that day shall not come, except there come a falling away first, and that man of sin be revealed, the son of perdition.
7. **2 Thessalonians 2:6,7** — And now ye know what withholdeth that he might be revealed in his time. For the mystery of iniquity doth already work: only he who now letteth will let, until he be taken out of the way.
8. **2 Thessalonians 2:8** (*NKJV*) — And then the lawless one will be revealed....

GREEK WORDS

1. "salt" — **ἅλας** (*halas*): one of the most expensive and valuable commodities in the ancient world; the phrase "worth your salt" was a term used to describe a person's value; in the Roman military, soldiers were partially paid in salt, and it indicated a person was deserving of his salary or wages; salt was principally used in seven ways — to depict what is valuable, as a preservative, as a flavor enhancer, as an antiseptic, as a medicinal and healing agent, to give protection from and to drive away evil spirits, and as a fertilizer

2. "good" — καλός (*kalos*): attractive; beneficial; wonderful
3. "saltiness" — ἄναλος (*analos*): bland; flat; insipid; tasteless; unsalty
4. "have" — ἔχω (*echo*): to have, to hold, and to possess
5. "withholdeth" — κατέχω (*katecho*): to hold fast; to hold down; to hold back; to suppress; to restrain; to hinder

SYNOPSIS

In Matthew 5:13, Jesus said, "Ye are the salt of the earth...." Many people read this verse and immediately move on, not pondering the weight of this profound statement made by Jesus. But in the New Testament world, salt was extremely valuable and rare. In fact, there were seven primary uses for salt. In this lesson, we will closely examine the first two: to express great value and to act as a preservative.

The emphasis of this lesson:

Salt was a rare and precious commodity in Jesus' day. Hence, the primary use of salt was to express value for something or someone. Salt was also used as a preservative to keep things from going bad. As believers, our influence and presence are a preserving force in the world, warding off rot and ruin and restraining evil.

A Review of Lesson 1

Jesus called us the salt of the earth in the synoptic gospels of Matthew, Mark, and Luke. In Mark 9:50, Jesus said, "Salt is good: but if the salt have lost his saltness, wherewith will ye season it? Have salt in yourselves...."The word "salt" that appears twice in this passage is the Greek word *halas*, and it depicts one of the most expensive and valuable commodities in the ancient world. The phrase "worth your salt" was a term used to describe a person's value.

Salt was principally used in seven different ways in the ancient world. Along with depicting what is valuable, salt was used as a preservative, as a flavor enhancer, as an antiseptic, as a medicinal and healing agent, to give protection from and to drive away evil spirits, and as a fertilizer. Interestingly, Roman soldiers were partially paid in salt, and to say a soldier was "worth his salt" was to indicate he was deserving of his salary or wages.

In the mind of the First Century hearers, when Jesus said, "You are the salt of the earth," suddenly all the common uses for salt came to their minds. They were already familiar with salt's many functions, and in their minds, it was good. The fact that Jesus called His followers salt and then said, "Salt is good," means He was calling them — and *us* — good.

The word "good" in Mark 9:50 describes *something attractive, beneficial, or wonderful*. In Greek, the word "good" is a form of the word *kalos*. Its use here means that if we're functioning as the salt of the earth as Jesus called us to be, then we're making the Gospel more attractive. Likewise, when we bring the benefits of the Gospel to people, people think the Gospel is just wonderful.

In contrast, Jesus went on to say, "…But if the salt have lost his saltness, wherewith will ye season it?" (Mark 9:50.) The word "saltness" in Greek is a form of the word *analos*, which describes that which is *bland, flat, insipid, tasteless*, or *unsalty*. As believers filled with the fire of the Holy Spirit, we are not supposed to be bland, flat, insipid, tasteless, or unsalty. We are supposed to be so salty that we make others want to have what we have.

Jesus commanded us, "…Have salt in yourselves…" (Mark 9:50). The word "have" here is a form of the Greek word *echo*, and it means *to have, to hold*, and *to possess*. Hence, Jesus wants us to have salt, to hold salt, and to possess salt in ourselves. Everything about us should be like salt, and the effects of salt should be produced in and through our lives. It is difficult to try and regain "saltness" once it is lost.

Salt Was Rare and Was Used To Express Value

Salt was very valuable, which brings us to the first main use for salt: to *express value for something or someone*. When Jesus said, "You are the salt of the earth," this was the equivalent of Him saying, "You are valuable! You're worth big bucks. You are the salt of the earth, and you are a treasure!" That's what Jesus says when He looks at *you*. You are cherished and treasured by God.

As we've noted, salt in the ancient world was a rare commodity and not easily accessible. Thus, it was rarely used, and when it was used, it was applied carefully and sparingly. High quality salt could only be found in a few places in Israel:

- The Hill of Salt — a seven-mile stretch located on the southwest coast of the Dead Sea.
- The marshes that were situated along the banks of the Dead Sea.
- The salt pits that were near the Dead Sea.

The process of collecting and processing the salt from these locations was laborious and elaborate; therefore, it was very expensive to yield the final product. Again, this made salt very valuable. Jesus was aware of all these dynamics when He said that we, His devoted followers, are the salt of the earth. It was His way of attaching great worth to us in a way the people of His day could easily understand.

You Are an Extraordinary Treasure!

If you have ever doubted how valuable you are to God, take time to really reflect on First Peter 1:18 and 19. In this verse, God declares through the apostle Peter the exceedingly high price Jesus paid to cover the penalty for your sin and to buy you back from Satan's slave market. Peter wrote:

> **Forasmuch as ye know that ye were not redeemed with corruptible things, as silver and gold, from your vain conversation received by tradition from your fathers; but with the precious blood of Christ, as of a lamb without blemish and without spot.**

Friend, you were redeemed with the precious blood of Jesus. There was no greater price ever paid than the price He paid for you! And Jesus was willing to pay the extraordinary price of His own life's blood because He deemed you to be that valuable!

The apostle John also spoke about the extraordinary value God has placed on our lives. Writing under the anointing of the Holy Spirit, John declared:

> **Behold, what manner of love the Father hath bestowed upon us, that we should be called the sons of God....**
> **— 1 John 3:1**

Along with John and Peter, the apostle Paul also wrote about how valuable we are to the Father, telling us:

> **But we have this treasure in earthen vessels, that the excellency of the power may be of God, and not of us.**
> **— 2 Corinthians 4:7**

The word "treasure" in this verse is a form of the Greek word *thesauros*, which describes *a luxurious treasure room where treasures were kept*. This word *thesauros* often brings to mind the lavish treasure houses of the pharaohs of Egypt. Those treasure chambers are filled with riches beyond imagination.

If you've ever watched an old movie where people are searching for lost treasure, the map they are using often has a big "X" marking where the treasure is located. Well, if "X" marks the spot for where the treasure is, then — in our case — the "X" would be on us! We are God's divine treasure chamber — His *thesauros* — and deep inside us, He has deposited all the riches of Christ Jesus in the form of His Holy Spirit. This includes the gifts of the Spirit as well as the fruit of the Spirit.

Again, Paul said, "But we have this treasure in earthen vessels…" (2 Corinthians 4:7). In other words, we are jam-packed and overflowing with all of God's goodness! That is why Jesus declared that we are the salt of the earth.

By faith, you need to grab hold of the great value God the Father and Jesus His Son have placed upon you. You can wrap your arms around this truth and make it your own by opening your mouth and declaring, "I am the salt of the earth! Jesus paid for me with His own precious blood, and I am called a child of God. He has deposited in me all the indescribable treasures of Christ in the person of the Holy Spirit."

Salt Was Used as a Preservative

Another major use for salt was as a preservative. Specifically, salt was used to preserve meats and other kinds of perishable foods. In the warm temperatures in Israel, meat would quickly begin to spoil, decay, and rot. However, when salt was added even in small measures, it preserved the meat.

When the people in Jesus' day heard Him say, "You are the salt of the earth," they instinctively knew salt was a preservative to keep things from going bad. Hence, they understood that He was telling us our influence and our presence have preserving power. Wherever we are in the world, we should be a preserving force against decay.

Let's face it: Ever since sin made its entrance into the world through Adam and Eve's disobedience, everything has been in breakdown mode. Scientists call this *entropy* or the Second Law of Thermodynamics.

Everything is in a state of decay. Ultimately, when Jesus returns, He will reverse this curse and make everything right again.

Until that time, we are the **salt** of the earth that wards off ruin, rot, and decay. Christ in us is the hope of God's glory (*see* Colossians 1:27), working to preserve marriages and communities and promote healing and restoration wherever we go. God's presence in us should stop the advancement of depravity and decadence.

That is why Jesus said, "...Have *salt* in yourselves..." (Mark 9:50). In other words, "Be like salt." As we live in relationship with God — allowing His Word to dwell in us richly and abiding in fellowship with the Holy Spirit — it causes us to be like salt. Then our very presence helps to reduce the corruption that is eating away at the fabric of society. In fact, as long as we are in the world as God's holy people, our presence should keep the world from going totally off the deep end into full-blown evil.

As the 'Salt of the Earth,' We Are the 'Restrainer' of Evil

If there was one overarching reason for us to be the salt of the earth in our present day, it is to function as the great "restrainer" that the apostle Paul described in Second Thessalonians 2. In this chapter, Paul prophesied that, at the very end of the age, corruption will reach an all-time high, but it will be held in check by an unseen force. Beginning in verse 3, Paul said:

> **Let no man deceive you by any means: for that day shall not come, except there come a falling away first, and that man of sin be revealed, the son of perdition.**
> **— 2 Thessalonians 2:3**

Under the inspiration of the Holy Spirit, Paul was describing a worldwide mutiny against God and His Word. The words "falling away" in the original Greek text depict such a mutiny, and we are experiencing this right now in our present day.

When we factor in the original Greek meaning of the key words in this verse, the *Renner Interpretive Version* (*RIV*) of Second Thessalonians 2:3 is as follows:

> **In light of these things, I urge you to refuse to allow anyone to take advantage of you. For example, you won't need a letter to**

tell you when the day of the Lord has come. You ought to know by now that this day can't come until first a worldwide insurgency, rebellion, riot, and mutiny against God has come about in society. Once that occurs, the world will be primed, prepared, and ready to embrace the Man of Lawlessness, the one who hates law and has rebellion running in his blood. This is the long-awaited and predicted Son of Doom and Destruction, the one who brings rot and ruin to everything he touches. When the time is just right, he will finally come out of hiding and go public.

Through the apostle Paul, the Holy Spirit prophesied that, at the very end of the age, in the last of the last days, there is going to be a worldwide insurgency, rebellion, riot, and mutiny against God in society. What is stopping this full-fledged rebellion from manifesting on the world scene? Paul told us in Second Thessalonians 2:6, which says:

And now ye know what withholdeth that he might be revealed in his time.

Notice the word "withholdeth." It is a form of the Greek word *katecho*, a compound of the words *kata* and *echo*. The word *kata* is a preposition that means *down* and carries the idea of *something dominating or subjugating*. The word *echo* means *to have*, *to hold*, and *to possess*. When these two words are joined to form *katecho*, it means *to hold fast*; *to hold down*; *to hold back*; *to suppress*; *to restrain*; or *to hinder*.

The use of this word *katecho* — translated here as "withholdeth"— tells us there is a suppressing, restraining, hindering force on the earth right now that is stopping the manifestation of the "son of perdition," which is another name for the antichrist.

Factoring in the original Greek meaning of the key words in this verse, here is the *Renner Interpretive Version* (*RIV*) of Second Thessalonians 2:6:

Now in light of everything I've told you before, you ought to be well aware by now that there is a supernatural force at work that is preventing the materialization of this person and the disclosure of his identity. This restraining force I'm referring to is so strong that it is currently putting on the brakes and holding back the unveiling of this wicked person, stalling and postponing his manifestation. But when the right moment

comes, this evil one will no longer be withheld, and he will
emerge on the world scene! The screen that has been hiding his
true identity and guarding him from world view will suddenly
be pulled back and evaporate — and he will step out on center
stage to let everyone know who he is.

What is this invisible, restraining force? It is us! More specifically, it is
the Holy Spirit of God in us, the Church. As Jesus said in Matthew 5:13,
we are the *salt of the earth*! His Spirit in us is acting as a preserving force
that is holding back the full flood of ruin, rot, decay, and a level of evil this
world has not yet seen.

In Second Thessalonians 2:7, Paul went on to say:

For the mystery of iniquity doth already work: only he who now
letteth will let, until he be taken out of the way.

The phrase "he who now letteth" is us, the Church. Through Paul, the
Holy Spirit is telling us that at some point the Church — that's us — will
be taken out of the way. This is what is known as the Rapture.

Factoring in the original Greek meaning of the key words in this verse,
here is the *Renner Interpretive Version (RIV)* of Second Thessalonians 2:7:

These events have been covertly in the making for a long time,
but the world doesn't realize that a secret plan is being executed
right under their own noses. The only thing that has kept this
plan from already being consummated is the supernatural
force that has been holding it all back until now. But one day
this force will be removed from the picture — and when that
happens, these events will quickly transpire.

Friend, the Church of the Lord Jesus Christ is the supernatural force
holding back the advancement of evil. As the SALT of the earth, we are
preserving the sanity of humanity from being fully engulfed by evil and
corruption. But one day, the Church will be removed from the picture.
When that happens, all hell will literally begin to break loose on the earth.
The Bible says:

And then the lawless one will be revealed....
— 2 Thessalonians 2:8 (*NKJV*)

The Greek text actually says, "In that very synchronized moment when the Church is removed and the great preserving force is no longer present, then the Lawless One will be revealed."

When we factor in the original Greek meaning of the key words in this verse, the *Renner Interpretive Version (RIV)* of Second Thessalonians 2:8 is as follows:

> **The removal of this restraining force will signal the moment when the Lawless One will finally make his grand appearance to the world.**

Friend, as long as we, the Church, are on this earth, keeping salt in ourselves and acting as a preserving force against ruin, rot, and wickedness, the antichrist cannot manifest. That is how strong we are as a preserving force.

So continue to "have salt in yourself" (Mark 9:50). Be God's preserving force in your family, on your job, and in your community. Through you, the Spirit of God will hold back corruption and evil until the day we are all raptured away.

STUDY QUESTIONS

> **Study to shew thyself approved unto God, a workman that needeth not to be ashamed, rightly dividing the word of truth.**
> **— 2 Timothy 2:15**

1. Peter told us that we were not redeemed with silver and gold but with *the precious blood of Christ (see* 1 Peter 1:18,19). What do you know about the blood of Jesus? Are there any specific verses that come to mind? Check out these verses which all punctuate the value and power of the Blood:

   • Matthew 26:28

   • Romans 5:9

   • Hebrews 9:14

   • Hebrews 10:19-22

   • First John 1:7; Revelation 1:5

   • Revelation 12:11

2. You are God's divine treasure chamber! Deep inside you, He has deposited all the *riches of Christ Jesus* in the Person of the Holy Spirit. What do these riches include? Explore these passages to discover some of the amazing treasures God has placed in you!

   • **The nine gifts of the Spirit** – First Corinthians 12:7-11

   • **The nine fruit of the Spirit** – Galatians 5:22 and 23

   • **The fullness of Christ** – First Corinthians 1:30; Colossians 2:2,3,9,10

   • **Everything you need** – Ephesians 1:3; Second Peter 1:3,4

PRACTICAL APPLICATION

> But be ye doers of the word, and not hearers only,
> deceiving your own selves.
> — James 1:22

1. As believers, we are called to be a preserving force that wards off rot, ruin, and decay. Are you functioning in this way? If so, how is your life protecting and keeping your loved ones, your coworkers, and the people in your community from decay? Who has God used in your life to help preserve you, your marriage, and your family?

2. Take some time to reread the *Renner Interpretive Version* (*RIV*) of Second Thessalonians 2:3,6,7, and 8. What is God showing you about the presence of us — His Church — on the earth and how His Spirit in us is holding back sin and wickedness? How does the meaning of these verses in the original Greek help you better understand the end of days and the coming of the antichrist?

3. God's Spirit in us is acting as the great "restrainer" in the earth, holding back the full flood of depravity, evil, and lawlessness that's trying to engulf the world. But one day soon we will be removed in an event called the *rapture of the Church*. According to First Thessalonians 4:15-17 and First Corinthians 15:51-53, what will this event be like?

TOPIC

Salt Was Used as a Flavor Enhancer and Salt Was Used as an Antiseptic

SCRIPTURES

1. **Matthew 5:13** — Ye are the salt of the earth....
2. **Mark 9:50** — Salt is good: but if the salt have lost his saltness, wherewith will ye season it? Have salt in yourselves....
3. **Colossians 4:6** — Let your speech be always with grace, seasoned with salt....
4. **Titus 2:9,10** — Exhort servants to be obedient unto their own masters, and to please them well in all things; not answering again; not purloining, but shewing all good fidelity; that they may adorn the doctrine of God our Saviour in all things.
5. **1 Peter 3:15** — But sanctify the Lord God in your hearts: and be ready always to give an answer to every man that asketh you a reason of the hope that is in you with meekness and fear.
6. **Matthew 28:19,20** (*NKJV*) — Go therefore and make disciples of all the nations, baptizing them in the name of the Father and of the Son and of the Holy Spirit, teaching them to observe all things that I have commanded you; and lo, I am with you always, even to the end of the age. Amen.

GREEK WORDS

1. "salt" — ἅλας (*halas*): one of the most expensive and valuable commodities in the ancient world; the phrase "worth your salt" was a term used to describe a person's value; in the Roman military, soldiers were partially paid in salt, and it indicated a person was deserving of his salary or wages; salt was principally used in seven ways — to depict what is valuable, as a preservative, as a flavor enhancer, as an antiseptic, as a medicinal and healing agent, to give protection from and to drive away evil spirits, and as a fertilizer
2. "good" — καλός (*kalos*): attractive; beneficial; wonderful

3. "saltness" — **ἄναλος** (*analos*): bland; flat; insipid; tasteless; unsalty
4. "have" — **ἔχω** (*echo*): to have, to hold, and to possess
5. "adorn" — **κοσμέω** (*kosmeo*): to adorn; to decorate; where we get the word cosmetics
6. "be ready always" — **ἀεὶ** (*aei*): always, perpetually, or unceasingly
7. "to give an answer" — **ἀπολογία** (*apologia*): a compound of **ἀπό** (*apo*) and the word **λόγος,** (*logos*); the word **ἀπό** (*apo*) means back, as to respond or to return, and the word **λόγος,** (*logos*) means word and can refer to words that are either spoken or written; as a compound, it depicts one who gives an answer to someone; a legal term used to denote a legal trial where one is put on the witness stand to give a defense of himself; it describes not only an answer, but an answer that is defendable; this clearly means believers should know what they believe well enough to intelligently defend it when they are put on trial by unbelievers, skeptics, or those who question what they believe

SYNOPSIS

In Matthew 5:13, Jesus said, "Ye are the salt of the earth…." This is a profound declaration that is loaded with meaning. In our last lesson, we learned that when Jesus called us the salt of the earth, He was telling us that we are very *valuable* and one of the most important commodities on the earth.

Instead of putting yourself down and allowing the enemy to badger you with condemnation, begin seeing yourself as the cherished treasure God says you are. According to First Peter 1:18 and 19, you were not redeemed with silver or gold, but by the precious blood of Jesus Christ.

Second Corinthians 4:7 says that you carry within you a divine "treasure," and the Greek word for "treasure" is a form of *thesauros*, which is where we get the word "thesaurus." If you've ever used a thesaurus, you know it's a treasury of words on top of words that are all used to describe one thing. By using the word "thesauros" in this verse, Paul was telling us that there are not enough words in the human vocabulary to describe the amazing treasure that is in you.

The instant you repented of your sin and received Christ into your life, you became *a treasure chamber*. That is what the word *thesauros* means. In that divine moment, you were born again into the family of God, and He made an indescribable deposit of all the riches of Christ inside you. You are now the house of the Holy Spirit, and you carry Him everywhere you go. You have the fullness of the gifts of the Spirit, the fruit of the Spirit, and all that Christ is inside you. Indeed, you are a walking treasure chamber! You are the salt of the earth!

The emphasis of this lesson:

As the salt of the earth, we are to add flavor to everything in life. Our attitudes, words, and actions — even our very presence — should improve the "taste" of society and our surroundings wherever we go. We are also to serve as a spiritual antiseptic in our sin-sick world and stop the spread of disease.

In the Ancient World
Salt Was of Great Value

In addition to Jesus calling us the "salt of the earth" in Matthew 5:13, He also said, "Salt is good: but if the salt have lost his saltness, wherewith will ye season it? Have salt in yourselves…" (Mark 9:50). As we have seen, the word "salt" is the Greek word *halas*, and it describes one of the most expensive and valuable commodities in antiquity.

In fact, the phrase "worth your salt" was a term used during the First Century to describe a person's value. Still today, some people will say, "He's really worth his salt," which means he is worth every penny he is being paid. In the Roman military, soldiers were partially paid in salt, which indicated they were deserving of their salary or wages.

Salt was primarily used seven ways in ancient times:

1. To depict what is valuable

2. As a preservative

3. As a flavor enhancer

4. As an antiseptic

5. As a medicinal and healing agent

6. To give protection from and to drive away evil spirits

7. As a fertilizer

When Jesus compared us to salt, He was connecting us with all these amazing qualities. These are the good things for which salt was known and the benefits it provided. When He said, "Salt is good," the Greek word for "good" is a form of *kalos*, which describes *something that is attractive, beneficial, and wonderful.*

Essentially, this means that wherever you are, if you're being the salt of the earth as Jesus called you to be, you will be advantageous to all those around you. Your lifestyle and the way you speak and live will make the Gospel more attractive. Your very presence will be beneficial to whoever is with you, and when you show up, people will say, "Wow! Isn't it wonderful that he or she is here?" That's what happens when you're doing your job as the salt of the earth.

"…But if the salt have lost his saltness, wherewith will ye season it?" (Mark 9:50.) Again, that is what Jesus said, and we have seen that the word "saltness" is a form of the Greek word *analos*, which means *that which is bland, flat, insipid, tasteless*, or *saltless.* These words should never be used to describe you. As a Christian, you never want to be seen as bland, monotonous, flat, tasteless, or unsalty.

It is God's will that you be *salty*, which is why Jesus said, "…Have salt in yourselves…" (Mark 9:50). The word "have" is a form of the Greek word *echo*, which means *to have, to hold*, and *to possess.* The Lord wants you to have salt, to hold salt, and to possess all the various qualities of salt in yourself. Likewise, God wants you to be so salty that when people get around you, they want more of what you have.

You Are Just Like Salt — Rare and Highly Valued

Salt in the ancient world was a rare commodity that was highly valued, seldom wasted, and sparingly used. This very expensive and treasured product was crucial and needed in many spheres of life. The same is true about you. Jesus calls you the *salt of the earth*, and by doing so, He is saying you are a treasured commodity that is needed in many spheres of life. Truly, you are cherished by God.

High-quality salt could only be found in a few places in Israel:

- The Hill of Salt — a seven-mile stretch located on the southwest coast of the Dead Sea.

- The marshes that were situated along the banks of the Dead Sea.
- The salt pits that were near the Dead Sea.

In each of these locations, the collecting of salt was an expensive process that was very elaborate and laborious. This placed a very high value on salt, making it very costly, which is a fact you need to keep in mind, as it will help you understand why Jesus calls you the salt of the earth.

Just as a great deal of work and expense went into finding and refining salt, a great deal of work and expense went into saving you. Your salvation was very costly for Jesus — it cost His very life. Not only was His blood poured out for you, but also His Spirit has been poured into you, and He has been working tirelessly to sanctify you and transform you into the likeness of Jesus.

That's why you should never badger yourself or put yourself down when you stumble and fall. Instead, you should say, "I'm the salt of the earth, and I'm very costly to Jesus. Regardless of what the enemy or others say or how I feel about myself, it doesn't change my value."

Salt Is a Flavor-Enhancer

In addition to expressing value and acting as a preservative, salt is one of the most profound flavor enhancers that exists in the culinary world. A person quickly becomes aware when food lacks salt, because food that does not have salt is often bland, monotonous, and uninteresting. But when just a little pinch of salt is added, the food is suddenly ignited with flavor.

Have you ever had French fries that came right out of the fryer and were well-seasoned with salt? Although these popular potato wedges are not the healthiest thing to eat, they sure do taste good! But what would French fries taste like if you didn't put any salt on them? They'd be rather bland, boring, insipid, and monotonous.

Well, just as salt was used in the ancient world to give food a stronger, richer flavor and was considered essential for the enhancement of taste, you are the salt of the earth that adds flavor to everything in life. Your very presence should change the flavor of society and your surroundings wherever you go.

Our Words and Actions
Are Meant To Enhance the World Around Us

One of the primary ways we enhance the "flavor" of the world around us is through our words. The apostle Paul zeroed in on this in his letter to the believers in Colossae. He said, "Let your speech be always with grace, seasoned with salt…" (Colossians 4:6).

This means that, instead of speaking negative, critical words or complaining with the rest of the world, you can exert a strong spiritual influence into your environment by speaking positive words that are *seasoned with salt*. In other words, speak words that bring preservation, promote healing, and add value. You can also use your words to enhance the flavor of what would otherwise be a very negative situation. This is what it means to "Let your speech be always with grace, seasoned with salt…" (Colossians 4:6).

God's intention is for you to have an enhancing effect on the world around you, improving the taste of everything. Paul also addressed the way we speak in Titus 2:9 and 10, where he says, "Exhort servants to be obedient unto their own masters, and to please them well in all things; not answering again; not purloining, but shewing all good fidelity; that they may adorn the doctrine of God our Saviour in all things."

In this passage, the word "adorn" is a form of the Greek word *kosmeo*, which means *to adorn* or *to decorate*. It is where we get the word "cosmetics." The phrase "adorn the doctrine of God" means to do what is right and to honor God in what we say and how we say it. This decorates the Gospel and enhances its flavor so that it is very inviting and tasty to people's souls.

In fact, if we're really doing a good job of being salt, our lives will make people thirsty for what we have. If you've ever eaten something with a lot of salt, you know the salt makes you thirsty. In the same way, our very presence should make people thirsty for the Lord.

We Are To Always Be Ready
To Give an Answer for the Hope We Have

Without question, the world around us has become unpredictable, crazy, and quite scary. People are looking for answers, and as Christ's ambassadors, we need to be ready to share with others the reason for the hope we have. The apostle Peter said it this way:

> **But sanctify the Lord God in your hearts: and be ready always to give an answer to every man that asketh you a reason of the hope that is in you with meekness and fear.**
> **— 1 Peter 3:15**

Notice the phrase "be ready always." It is a translation of the Greek word *aei*, and it means *always, perpetually*, or *unceasingly*. Thus, we could translate this part of the verse, "*...Always, perpetually, and unceasingly be ready to give an answer to every man that asks you a reason of the hope that is in you with meekness and fear.*"

The words "to give an answer" are derived from a form of the Greek word *apologia*, a compound of *apo* and the word *logos*. The word *apo* means *back*, such as *to respond* or *to return*, and the word *logos* means *words* and can refer to *words that are either spoken or written*. When these two words are compounded to form the new word *apologia*, it depicts *one who gives an answer to someone*.

Interestingly, the word *apologia* was a legal term used to denote a legal trial where one is put on the witness stand to give a defense of himself. It describes not only an answer, but an answer that is defendable. This clearly means believers should know what they believe well enough to intelligently defend it when they are put on trial by unbelievers, skeptics, or those who question what they believe.

When we factor in the original Greek meaning of the key words in this verse, the *Renner Interpretive Version* (*RIV*) of First Peter 3:15 is as follows:

> **But it's essential for you to consecrate, dedicate, and set apart a specially sanctified and hallowed place for Christ within your heart — that is, at the core of your very being and the part of you that affects everything in your life. And just like runners do all that is needed to prepare and train in advance to run a race — or like soldiers, whose preparation and training makes them ready to spring into action at a moment's notice — you must do all you can to be ready and to stay in a perpetual state of preparedness at all times to intelligently answer and defend the truth for absolutely everyone who insists to hear an intelligent explanation about the things that have to do with your expectations and hopes, answering those who seek answers with the attitude and demeanor of forbearance, meekness, and patience and remaining in control of yourself even if they insult you or speak in an ugly**

manner. Your goal is to answer them in such a way that it brings a soothing presence that calms angry or upset souls, or that brings peace into troublesome or unsettling situations, and it is needful for you to also answer the inquirer with a sense of concern and seriousness for them.

We Are Called To Be an Antiseptic, Stopping the Spread of Disease, Malfunction, and Collapse

Not only are we meant to enhance the lives of others but also to serve as an *antiseptic*. In the ancient world, dirt and disease were common enemies, and salt was used as an antiseptic, especially in very unclean or contaminated areas. It was believed that if you just doused salt on an area, it would work as a disinfectant.

History documents that if sickness began to spread throughout a village, those trying to stop its spread would vacate the village, relocate all the sick people, and when the village was finally emptied, they would begin to disperse salt throughout the entire region. They believed salt acted like a disinfectant.

When Jesus calls us the salt of the earth, it means we are to be like an antiseptic and have a disinfecting presence wherever we go. Medically speaking, salt was viewed as a bacteriostat, an agent that inhibited bacteria from multiplying. Specifically, it inhibited the kind of bacteria that provoked enzymes that caused a malfunction and ultimately a complete collapse.

Therefore, if we are functioning as salt like Jesus has called us to function, our very presence should act like a bacteriostat, stopping malfunction and keeping things from collapsing. This is part of the Great Commission Christ gave us. He said:

> Go therefore and make disciples of all the nations, baptizing them in the name of the Father and of the Son and of the Holy Spirit, teaching them to observe all things that I have commanded you; and lo, I am with you always, even to the end of the age. Amen.
>
> — Matthew 28:19,20 (*NKJV*)

Friend, God has called you to be the salt of the earth, which includes acting like a bacteriostat. He has energized you with the power of the Holy Spirit and equipped you with His Word and the blood of Jesus to stop malfunction and collapse in society. You are His antiseptic for a sick world.

So along with being a flavor enhancer in the world, we have also been called to be a spiritual antiseptic. Wherever we go, we are to be a spiritual disinfectant that removes the sickening effects of sin and prevents disease, malfunction, and collapse. Our very presence should be a saving, delivering presence.

Again, Jesus said, "Ye are the salt of the earth..." (Matthew 5:13).

- Salt is valuable, so *you are valuable.*
- Salt is a preserving force, so *you should be a preserving force wherever you go.*
- Salt is a flavor enhancer, so *you should add flavor to life and people wherever you are.*
- Salt is an antiseptic, so *you should be like an antiseptic that disinfects and stops the spread of disease, harm, and destruction wherever you go.*

That is how powerful you are in Christ. Your life should be so salty that people begin to thirst for the person of Jesus whose Spirit is living inside you. All this meaning is packed in this phrase, "You are the salt of the earth."

STUDY QUESTIONS

Study to shew thyself approved unto God, a workman that needeth not to be ashamed, rightly dividing the word of truth.
— 2 Timothy 2:15

1. In this lesson, we learned that being the "salt of the earth" includes adding flavor to life. But did you know that your life — just like Jesus' life — gives off an aroma? You are an ambassador for Christ, and God is making His appeal to others through you. Take time to carefully reflect on these passages and write what the Holy Spirit shows you about the fragrance you emit to others.

   Follow God's example in everything you do just as a much loved child imitates his father. Be full of love for others, following

the example of Christ who loved you and gave himself to God as a sacrifice to take away your sins. And God was pleased, for Christ's love for you was like sweet perfume to him.
— Ephesians 5:1,2 (*TLB*)

Thanks be to God who leads us, wherever we are, on his own triumphant way and makes our knowledge of him spread throughout the world like a lovely perfume! We Christians have the unmistakable "scent" of Christ, discernible alike to those who are being saved and to those who are heading for death. To the latter it seems like the very smell of doom, to the former it has the fresh fragrance of life itself....
— 2 Corinthians 2:14-16 (*J.B. Phillips*)

So we are Christ's ambassadors, God making His appeal as it were through us. We [as Christ's personal representatives] beg you for His sake to lay hold of the divine favor [now offered you] and be reconciled to God.
— 2 Corinthians 5:20 (*AMPC*)

2. The quality of your words is one of the ways you can enhance the flavor of life and bless the people around you. How powerful are your words? And what happens to them after you speak them? Take a look at what the Bible says about the importance and blessings of taming your tongue:

   - **Your words are powerful** — Proverbs 18:21; Ecclesiastes 10:12

   - **You will eat your words** — Proverbs 12:14; 13:2; 18:20

   - **You will be blessed if you watch what you say** — Psalm 34:12-14; Proverbs 13:3; 21:23

   - **Mastering your mouth adds worth to your witness** — James 1:26; 3:2

   - **Never underestimate the power of your tongue** — James 3:1-12

   - **Consider David's and Isaiah's words as a prayer to guard your mouth** — Psalm 141:3; Isaiah 50:4

   We must let our attitudes, our actions, and our words enable people to "taste and see that the Lord is good..." (Psalm 34:8).

PRACTICAL APPLICATION

But be ye doers of the word, and not hearers only,
deceiving your own selves.
— James 1:22

1. One of the primary ways we enhance the flavor of the world around us is through our *words*. If you were to take an honest inventory of the things you say, what kinds of words most frequently come out of your mouth? Are they positive or negative? Critical or constructive? Grateful or ungrateful? In view of your answer, are you enhancing or diminishing the flavor of the lives of others?

2. God instructs us to "…Be ready always to give an answer to every man that asketh you a reason of the hope that is in you…" (1 Peter 3:15). If you had 60 seconds to candidly share how Jesus has personally changed your life, what would you say? If you had 30 seconds to share the bare-bone essentials of the Gospel (Good News about Jesus), how would you answer? If you don't have answers for these questions, get alone with God and ask the Holy Spirit to help you be ready to give a reason for the hope that is within you. Rest assured, there are people all around you that need Jesus, and He needs you to tell them about Him!

LESSON 4

TOPIC

Salt Was Used as a Medicinal and Healing Agent and To Protect From and To Drive Away Evil Spirits

SCRIPTURES

1. **Matthew 5:13** — Ye are the salt of the earth….

2. **Mark 9:50** — Salt is good: but if the salt have lost his saltness, wherewith will ye season it? Have salt in yourselves….

3. **Mark 16:17,18** — And these signs shall follow them that believe…. They shall lay hands on the sick, and they shall recover.

4. **Luke 10:19** — Behold, I give unto you power to tread on serpents and scorpions, and over all the power of the enemy: and nothing shall by any means hurt you.

5. **Ephesians 6:13** — Wherefore take unto you the whole armour of God, that ye may be able to withstand in the evil day, and having done all, to stand.

GREEK WORDS

1. "salt" — **ἅλας** (*halas*): one of the most expensive and valuable commodities in the ancient world; the phrase "worth your salt" was a term used to describe a person's value; in the Roman military, soldiers were partially paid in salt, and it indicated a person was deserving of his salary or wages; salt was principally used in seven ways — to depict what is valuable, as a preservative, as a flavor enhancer, as an antiseptic, as a medicinal and healing agent, to give protection from and to drive away evil spirits, and as a fertilizer

2. "good" — **καλός** (*kalos*): attractive; beneficial; wonderful

3. "saltness" — **ἄναλος** (*analos*): bland; flat; insipid; tasteless; unsalty

4. "have" — **ἔχω** (*echo*): to have, to hold, and to possess

5. "follow" — **παρακολουθέω** (*parakoloutheo*): a compound of **παρα** (*para*) and **ἀκολουθέω** (*akoloutheo*); the preposition **παρα** (*para*) means to be alongside, to be near, or to be in close proximity; the word **ἀκολουθέω** (*akoloutheo*) means to follow or to go somewhere with a person, as to accompany him on a trip; when compounded, as in this verse, the new word means to tirelessly accompany someone, to constantly be at the side of an individual, or to always be in close proximity with a person, like a faithful companion who is always at one's side

6. "believe" — **πιστεύω** (*pisteuo*): literally, that are believing

7. "sick" — **ἄρρωστος** (*arrostos*): derived from **ῥώννυμι** (*rhonnumi*), which means to be well, to be strong, to be in good health, or to possess a strong physical condition; when an "a" is placed in front of this word, it reverses the condition, and instead, the new word means to be in bad health or to possess a weak and broken condition; the image of a person so weak and sick that he has become critically ill; an invalid

8. "recover" — **καλῶς** (*kalos*): to be well, to be healthy, or to be in good shape

9. "behold" — **ἰδού** (*idou*) — bewilderment, shock, amazement, and wonder
10. "power" — **ἐξουσία** (*exousia*): delegated authority; influence
11. "tread" — **πατέω** (*pateo*): to walk; to trample
12. "on" — **ἐπάνω** (*epano*): above; on top of; over; a position that is superior
13. "serpents" — **ὄφις** (*ophis*): serpents; snakes; creatures that bite; snakes hid in the ruts in the road and were known to bite travelers
14. "scorpions" — **σκορπίος** (*skorpios*): scorpions; creatures that sting; scorpions hid in the ruts in the road and were known to sting travelers
15. "over" — **ἐπί** (*epi*): over; describes a superior position
16. "all" — **πᾶσαν** (*pasan*): an all-inclusive term meaning all, with nothing excluded
17. "enemy" — **ἐχθρός** (*echthros*): hate, hatred, or hostility; an enemy or opponent; animosity, antagonism, or enmity; those who are irreconcilable; enemies in a military conflict; hostile enemies
18. "nothing" — **οὐδέν** (*ouden*): absolutely nothing; nothing at all
19. "hurt" — **ἀδικέω** (*adikeo*): to harm, hurt, or injure
20. "withstand" — **ἀντιστῆναι** (*antistenai*): to stand against

SYNOPSIS

Throughout history, salt has been known for its wide range of medicinal properties. For example, gargling with warm salt water can soothe the sting of a sore throat. Soaking in a tub doused with Epsom salt can ease sore muscles and back pain. And for those dealing with heartburn, a teaspoon of baking soda, which is a type of salt, stirred into a glass of cold water can help reduce the irritation. What does this have to do with our being the "salt of the earth"? That is the focus of this vital lesson.

The emphasis of this lesson:

As the salt of the earth, our presence is to be like medicine, bringing healing to people who are sick or suffering in any area of their life. Similarly, as salt, our presence should provide deliverance, safety, and freedom to people experiencing oppressive, evil influences. Jesus has given us His own delegated authority over all the enemy's power.

What We've Learned So Far

In Matthew 5:13, Jesus declared, "Ye are the salt of the earth...." He then added in Mark's gospel, "Salt is good: but if the salt have lost his saltness, wherewith will ye season it? Have salt in yourselves..." (Mark 9:50). We have seen that the word "good" — the Greek word *kalos* — means *attractive*, *beneficial*, or *wonderful*.

The use of this word *kalos* means that when you are living like Jesus, you make Him and the Gospel *attractive* to the people with whom you're doing life. When you show up, they think it's wonderful because they see you as someone who is beneficial in their life.

Jesus said, "Salt is good…" (Mark 9:50).

In the ancient world, salt was one of the most expensive and valuable commodities. This tells us if you are the salt of the earth, you are a valuable commodity. You are worth big bucks in Jesus' eyes.

The phrase "worth your salt" was a term used to describe a person's value.

People still use this saying today. If someone has really done a great job, he is a benefit to his organization, and he is worth his salary, then someone might say, "This guy is really worth his salt." This wording comes from the Roman world. During that era, soldiers in the military were partially paid in salt because it was so valuable, and it indicated they were deserving of their salary or wages.

Salt was principally used in seven ways.

It was used to depict what is valuable and also served as a preservative, as a flavor enhancer, as an antiseptic, as a medicinal and healing agent, to give protection from and to drive away evil spirits, and as a fertilizer.

Embrace your identity as the salt of the earth.

The fact Jesus declared salt is *good* and He called YOU the salt of the earth means you need to stop badgering and nitpicking yourself when you make mistakes. You are still learning and growing in Christ, and God is not finished with you yet. If you've done wrong, repent and make things right with God. Then, instead of putting yourself down, begin to say what God says about you.

Open your mouth and declare:

- "I am the salt of the earth!" (*See* Matthew 5:13.)
- "I am a valuable commodity!"
- "Jesus paid for me with His life's blood, so I'm priceless!" (*See* 1 Peter 1:18,19.)
- "He believes I'm so valuable He poured the treasure of His Spirit into me!" (*See* 2 Corinthians 4:7.)

Friend, all these things and more are what Jesus says about you, and you are meant to be attractive, beneficial, and wonderful everywhere you go!

Our life is to be so "salty" that people thirst for what we have.

Jesus went on to say, "…But if the salt have lost his saltness, wherewith will ye season it?…" (Mark 9:50). The word "saltness" in Greek is a form of *analos*, and it describes *that which is bland, flat, insipid, tasteless, monotonous, and unsalty.*

What the Lord is telling us in this verse is that, as believers, we are *never* to be bland, and we are *never* to be flat. We are also not to be insipid, tasteless, or monotonous. Instead, we should be the life of the party. We carry within us the life of God, and we're to be so salty that we make other people want what we have.

Have salt in yourself.

Jesus wrapped up Mark 9:50 by saying, "…Have salt in yourselves…." The word "have" is a form of the Greek word *echo*, which means *to have, to hold,* and *to possess.* Christ is giving us a commandment that we, as believers, are to be salty. We are to have salt in ourselves and possess all the effects of salt in our life.

The qualities of salt we have examined that you are to exhibit include:

One: Salt was very valuable, so you are valuable.

Two: Salt was used as a preservative, so God intends for your very presence to have a preserving effect wherever you go. You are to help stop the spread of rot, decay, and corruption, and you are to be a restraining force that holds back evil.

Three: Salt was used as a flavor enhancer, so wherever you go, you should add flavor and spice to life because you carry the fruit of the Spirit and the goodness of the Gospel inside of you. You are to be salty.

Four: Salt was used as an antiseptic or a disinfectant that stopped the spread of disease. In the same way, everywhere you are, you should bring such a presence of divine salt that it stops the spread of disease and the work of the devil.

When Jesus' hearers heard Him say, "You are the salt of the earth," they would have understood all of this, because these were all ways salt was used in the First Century.

Salt Was Used as a Medicinal and Healing Agent

History documents that Greeks, Romans, and Egyptians all used salt to treat cuts, wounds, and skin irritations. It was an important ingredient for physicians and those employed in the field of medicine. Salt was also used as a healing agent. For example, if a person was severely wounded, salt was poured into the wound to sanitize the wound from germs, to stop the spread of infection, and to stop the bleeding, all of which helped to speed up the healing process.

It is a scientific fact that salt has healing properties. It causes wounds to heal more speedily, and in the ancient world where medication was very rare, salt was an indispensable product in every doctor's medical bag.

It seems to have been especially valuable in cases where there was an open wound. For that reason, in every home, in every business, in every public place, salt was kept close at hand for the treatment of open wounds or sores.

When the followers of Jesus heard Him say His people were to be *the salt of the earth*, they would have understood that He meant they were to be carriers of physical healing as well as mental and emotional healing for those who have been wounded in life.

Just think about all the people today who are walking around wounded in so many areas of their life. Some are trying to live with gaping, open wounds in their soul. The mental and emotional pain they are trying to manage is nonstop. As the salt of the earth, we are the carriers of God's healing, and we are to be readily available to release His healing virtue whenever possible.

The Sign of Healing
Should Accompany Us Regularly

This idea of being God's healing agent is seen very clearly in the words Jesus spoke just before His ascension into Heaven. He declared to His followers — both then and now:

> **And these signs shall follow them that believe…. They shall lay hands on the sick, and they shall recover.**
> **— Mark 16:17,18**

Notice the word "follow" in this passage. It is a form of the Greek word *parakoloutheo*, a compound of the words *para* and *akoloutheo*. The preposition *para* means *to be alongside, to be near,* or *to be in close proximity;* the word *akoloutheo* means *to follow or to go somewhere with a person,* as in *to accompany him on a trip.* When compounded, as in this verse, they form a new word — *parakoloutheo* — which means *to tirelessly accompany someone, to constantly be at the side of an individual,* or *to always be in close proximity with a person, like a faithful companion who is always at one's side.*

The fact that Jesus used the word *parakoloutheo* — translated here as "follow" — means He's telling us that the occurrence of people being healed shouldn't be a rare event or something that happens in our life occasionally. Rather, it should constantly be at our side. In fact, all the signs Jesus spoke of in Mark 16:17 and 18 should be our constant traveling companions. Everywhere we go, these signs should be with us — they should always be in close proximity to wherever we are.

Now, there is a condition that must be met to see these signs manifest. Jesus said they will follow and be the constant companion of those who *believe.* This word "believe" is a form of the Greek word *pisteuo*, which literally means *that are believing.* The verb tense here is ongoing, which means these people *are believing* and *engaging their faith.*

So rather than relying on what you believed 5, 10, or 20 years ago, you need to be actively using your faith right now. As you actively press in and believe God to produce the signs and wonders He speaks of in His Word, your faith will trigger the manifestation of the miraculous in real time.

We Are Meant To Bring Healing
to the Sickest People of All

In Mark 16:18, Jesus said, "…They shall lay hands on the sick, and they shall recover." The word "sick" here is a form of the Greek word *arrostos*. It is derived from the word *rhonnumi*, which means *to be well, to be strong, to be in good health*, or *to possess a strong physical condition*. In this case, an "a" is placed in front of the word, which reverses the condition. Thus, the new word *arrostos* means *to be in bad health* or *to possess a weak and broken condition*. This word depicts a person so weak and sick that he has become critically ill. It can even be translated as *an invalid*.

The "sick" who Jesus says we are to lay our hands on are the sickest people of all. God's intention is for such power to flow through you that even invalids will get well! Jesus said that those who believe He is the Healer, can lay hands on the sickest of all and see them recover."

In Greek, the word "recover" is a form of the word *kalos*, and it means *to be well, to be healthy*, or *to be in good shape*. As the salt of the earth, you are a medicinal and healing agent, and your very presence should bring healing to anyone who is sick or suffering in any realm of life. The fact is, the power of the Holy Spirit and the authority of Jesus' name have been given to us, and they are sufficient to bring healing to people.

Look around you. Are you seeing people getting physically, emotionally, and spiritually stronger because of your presence near them? If not, why? Maybe you need to be engaging your faith for divine healing to follow you wherever you go. That is what you can and should expect because you are the salt of the earth!

Salt Was Used To Give Protection From
and Drive Away Evil Spirits

In the ancient world, many believed salt was a repellent of evil and had a certain level of power to give protection from and drive away evil spirits. The ancients believed this so strongly that they would draw a boundary line with salt across the threshold of their house, believing that demons could not pass over it.

In New Testament times, Rome occupied the land of Israel, thereby giving the Jews an opportunity to observe the Romans practicing pagan rituals, including the practice of using salt to drive away evil spirits. Consequently, when they heard Jesus say, "You are the salt of the earth," they knew He was also inferring that, as His followers, our very presence should provide protection from and drive away evil spirits and evil influences. Friend, as the salt of the earth, your presence should bring deliverance, safety, and freedom to the people around you.

Jesus describes the devil-defeating power He's given us in Luke 10:19, where He declares:

> **Behold, I give unto you power to tread on serpents and scorpions, and over all the power of the enemy: and nothing shall by any means hurt you.**

When Jesus said, "behold," He used the Greek word *idou*, a word describing *bewilderment*, *shock*, *amazement*, and *wonder*. It is the equivalent of Him saying, "*Wow!* This is so amazing! Listen to what I am about to say." He then downloaded a truth that every believer really needs to understand and personally grab hold of.

Jesus Has Given Us His Authority Over All the Power of the Enemy

Jesus said, "…I give unto you power…" (Luke 10:19). The word "power" is a form of the Greek word *exousia*, and it describes *delegated authority* or *influence*. The Lord has delegated to us His very own authority to "tread on serpents and scorpions" (Luke 10:19). The word "tread" is a form of the Greek word *pateo*, which means *to walk* or *to trample*. Jesus delegated His authority to us *to walk on* and *trample on* serpents and scorpions.

Interestingly, even the word "on" is significant. It is the Greek word *epano*, which means *above*, *on top of*, or *over*. It describes *a position that is superior*. In this case, it is a superior position to that of "serpents." And the word "serpents" comes from a form of the Greek word *ophis*, which describes *serpents*, *snakes*, or *creatures that bite*. In biblical times, snakes hid in the ruts in the road and were known to bite travelers. This made many people afraid to travel.

Along with snakes, there were also "scorpions" in the ruts of the road. In Greek, "scorpions" is a form of the word *skorpios*, which describes *scorpions* or *creatures that sting*. Jesus said you have authority over these things that bite and over things that sting. In fact, He said you have authority *over all the power of the enemy*.

The word "over" is the Greek word *epi*, which means *over* and describes *a superior position*, and the word "all" — the Greek word *pasan* — is an all-inclusive term meaning *all, with nothing excluded*. Hence, Jesus has given us absolutely all authority, nothing excluded, over the enemy.

This brings us to the word "enemy," which is a form of *echthros* in Greek, and it means *hate, hatred*, or *hostility*. It can also be translated as *an enemy or opponent; animosity; antagonism;* or *enmity*. It depicts *those who are irreconcilable; enemies in a military conflict;* or *hostile enemies*. Jesus has given you absolutely all authority over your enemies, and nothing — the Greek word *ouden*, meaning *absolutely nothing* or *nothing at all* — shall hurt you. The word "hurt" is a form of *adikeo* in Greek, and it means *to harm, hurt*, or *injure*.

Jesus said He has given you absolutely all authority to walk on and trample on all the enemy's power, and nothing whatsoever will harm or injure you. That is the power you have in Christ because you are the salt of the earth.

Our Presence As 'Salt' Is Meant To Create Spiritual Barriers

You may be thinking, *What else do I need to know about the salt that was poured out as a boundary to keep out evil?* To answer that question, we turn to the words penned by the apostle Paul in Ephesians 6:13:

> **Wherefore take unto you the whole armour of God, that ye may be able to withstand in the evil day, and having done all, to stand.**

Notice the word "withstand." It is a translation of the Greek word *antistenai*, which means *to stand against*. The first part of the word, *anti*, means *against*, and the word *stenai* means *to stand*. Together, the word *antistenai* carries the idea of *resisting or pushing against*, which means our very presence should create spiritual barriers wherever we go. If any evil tries to cross the barrier, we have the authority to push it away. Like salt in ancient times, God's presence in us should keep evil out of our space.

Likewise, if you come near someone who has been battling evil activity in his or her life, evil should be repelled. Why? Because you are the salt of the earth, and like the salt in ancient times, you bring protection and drive evil out of the area.

All that meaning is in the word *salt*, and you carry all these things within you. That's why Jesus said in Mark 9:50, "…Have salt in yourselves…." You're to be like salt and carry its effects everywhere you go.

STUDY QUESTIONS

Study to shew thyself approved unto God, a workman that needeth not to be ashamed, rightly dividing the word of truth.
— 2 Timothy 2:15

1. Do you feel depleted of faith? You are not alone. The apostles felt the same way and asked Jesus to "increase their faith" (*see* Luke 17:5). The Bible identifies two primary ways to grow your faith in Romans 10:17 and Jude 20 (also *see* 1 Corinthians 14:4). What are these practices and what can you do to make room for them in your daily life?

2. Jesus said He has given you His very own delegated authority to maintain a superior position over all the power of the enemy and trample him under your feet (*see* Luke 10:19). What else does the Bible say about your God-given authority as a believer? Check out these powerful promises from God's Word:

    • Matthew 16:19 and 18:18-20

    • Matthew 28:18-20

    • Mark 16:15-18

    • John 14:12-14; 15:16

    • James 4:8; 1 Peter 5:8 and 9

PRACTICAL APPLICATION

But be ye doers of the word, and not hearers only, deceiving your own selves.
—James 1:22

1. Take some time to carefully reread the original Greek meaning of Jesus' declaration in Luke 10:19. What new insights is the Holy Spirit

showing you about the authority and power you have been given in Christ?

2. Look around you. Are you seeing people getting physically, emotionally, and spiritually stronger because of your presence near them? If not, why? Pray and ask the Lord, "What's missing in my life? Am I actively engaging my faith and believing for divine healing to follow me wherever I go? What do I need to *start* doing and what do I need to *stop* doing to see the promised signs of Mark 16:17 and 18 regularly manifest in and through my life?" Be still and listen. What is the Holy Spirit saying to you?

LESSON 5

TOPIC

Salt Was Used as Fertilizer

SCRIPTURES

1. **Matthew 5:13** — Ye are the salt of the earth....

2. **Mark 9:50** — Salt is good: but if the salt have lost his saltness, wherewith will ye season it? Have salt in yourselves....

3. **John 15:16** — Ye have not chosen me, but I have chosen you, and ordained you, that ye should go and bring forth fruit....

4. **Colossians 1:6** — [The gospel has] come unto you, as it is in all the world; and bringeth forth fruit, as it doth also in you....

GREEK WORDS

1. "salt" — **ἅλας** (*halas*): one of the most expensive and valuable commodities in the ancient world; the phrase "worth your salt" was a term used to describe a person's value; in the Roman military, soldiers were partially paid in salt, and it indicated a person was deserving of his salary or wages; salt was principally used in seven ways — to depict what is valuable, as a preservative, as a flavor enhancer, as an antiseptic, as a medicinal and healing agent, to give protection from and to drive away evil spirits, and as a fertilizer

2. "good" — **καλός** (*kalos*): attractive; beneficial; wonderful

3. "saltness" — ἄναλος (*analos*): bland; flat; insipid; tasteless; unsalty

4. "have" — ἔχω (*echo*): to have, to hold, and to possess

5. "chosen" — ἐκλέγομαι (*eklegomai*): from ἐκ (*ek*) and λέγω (*lego*); the word ἐκ (*ek*) means out, and λέγω (*lego*) means "I say"; literally, "Out, I say"; to call out, to select, to elect, or to choose; it is used to refer to individuals who were selected for a specific purpose; it conveys the idea of the privilege and honor of being chosen; it is so connected to the idea of privilege that those being selected should look upon themselves as honored, esteemed, and respected; importantly used by Paul in Ephesians 1:4

6. "ordained" — τίθημι (*tithemi*): to establish; to ordain; to purposely set in place

7. "bring forth" — φέρω (*phero*): to bear; to carry; pictures something that is being carried along, like a leaf being carried by a gust of wind or like the current in a river that carries something like a fallen branch; the leaf and branch have no inherent ability to move by themselves and will only be moved if the wind or current carries them along; a technical word that was used in ancient times to denote a ship whose sails were set to catch the wind

8. "fruit" — καρπός (*karpos*): the fruit of plants or trees; used to depict the fruit borne by a person's life; this fruit might include a person's deeds, actions, moral character, and behavior or the output of the person's work; in essence, the word describes the byproduct of a plant or tree or of a person's life

9. "bringeth forth fruit" — καρποφορέω (*karpophoreo*): to bear fruit; to bring forth fruit; to be carried into fruitfulness

SYNOPSIS

When you hear the word "salt," what comes to mind? Do you see a small glass container with a silver top sitting on the kitchen table filled with tiny white granules? Or maybe a blue cylindrical container embossed with a little girl toting a yellow umbrella? Indeed, salt is plentiful nowadays. In the year 2023 alone, the United States produced 42 million tons of salt.[1]

But in the First Century, salt was a rare and treasured commodity. When Jesus called us the "salt of the earth," He was declaring us to be a tremendous treasure. In fact, we are so valuable that He died on the Cross and shed His life's blood to pay the penalty for our sin and to restore our relationship with the Father. In this final lesson, we will learn how salt was used as a fertilizer and what that means to us as Christians.

The emphasis of this lesson:

As the salt of the earth, we are a divine fertilizer. When we're present and functioning as good, spiritual salt, the soil of society and people's souls should be enriched, enabling everything and everyone to be healthier, stronger, and more productive. Jesus has chosen and ordained you to produce abundant fruit.

A Quick Review of Lessons 1-4

Once more, we turn our attention to Jesus' words in Mark 9:50, where He said, "Salt is good: but if the salt have lost his saltness, wherewith will ye season it? Have salt in yourselves...."

Jesus declared, "Salt is good..." (Mark 9:50).

As we have seen, salt was one of the most expensive and valuable commodities in the ancient world. That is why Jesus compared us with salt. In that one word — salt — He attached high value to us and communicated that we have multiple meaningful functions.

When someone says, "He's worth his salt," that person is describing someone's value.

People still use this expression today, especially if someone has done a great job and they're a benefit to the organization. Anyone who is worth his salary is considered someone who is "really worth his salt." This saying originated between the First and Third Century, when people were paid in salt. In the Roman world, soldiers were partially paid in salt, and it indicated a person was deserving of his salary or wages.

Salt was principally used in seven ways.

One: Salt depicted something of great value. As the salt of the earth, you have great value.

Two: Salt was used as a preservative. As salt, you are a preserving force that holds back rot, ruin, and decay and works collectively with the Church to restrain evil and the manifestation of the antichrist.

Three: Salt was used as a flavor enhancer. Because you are the salt of the earth, your presence should add "spice" to life and remove anything bland, flat, or monotonous.

Four: Salt was used as an antiseptic or disinfectant, which means when you're present, sickness and disease in any form should be held at bay and unable to spread.

Five: Salt was used as a medicinal and healing agent, especially to help heal open wounds. This means if you know someone who is physically sick or has been hurt in a relationship and has a gaping open wound in his or her soul, when you show up, your very presence should be a medicinal and healing agent to that person, helping to speed up the healing process.

Six: Salt was used to provide protection from and to drive away evil spirits. In ancient times, people believed if they put salt across the threshold of their house, evil could not penetrate their space. Similarly, if you're doing your job as the salt of the earth, you carry within you the delivering power of Jesus Christ, and wherever you go, evil cannot enter.

If evil spirits try to enter where you are, according to Ephesians 6:13, you have the power to push them back. In Christ, you have been given the might of His Name, the strength of His Word, and the power of His Holy Spirit. Furthermore, Luke 10:19 says that Jesus has given you a superior position and authority over all the power of the enemy, and nothing shall by any means hurt you.

The **seventh** way salt was used in the ancient world was as a fertilizer.

Salt Was Known as a Magnificent Fertilizer

For many years, farmers used salt to enrich and fertilize the soil on their farms in order to produce larger crops of a higher quality. Even a small amount of salt scattered sparingly on the ground could improve the quality of the soil and result in a bigger harvest and healthier crops.

Salt was viewed as an essential ingredient in the farming industry, and the best salt available at that time nourished and stimulated the earth to produce better crops. Jesus was aware of salt's use as a magnificent fertilizer.

What is interesting is that when He said, "Ye are the salt of the earth" in Matthew 5:13, the original Greek text actually says, "You are the salt of the *soil*." Amazingly, just as salt in the natural world stimulated the earth to yield better and bigger crops, when we are present and functioning as good, spiritual salt, things become more productive.

The implication here is that through our influence, the world in which we live should be better, and our very presence should make things become more productive. As believers, we carry within us God's divine presence, which — like salt — improves the quality of life and enhances productivity.

So as the salt of the earth, you are a divine fertilizer. Wherever you show up, the soil of society and people's souls should be enriched, enabling everything and everyone to be healthier, stronger, and more productive.

Jesus Has 'Chosen' You for a Purpose!

Jesus underscores this idea of fruitfulness and productivity in His discussion with His disciples in John 15:16, where He said:

> **Ye have not chosen me, but I have chosen you, and ordained you, that ye should go and bring forth fruit….**

According to this verse, all believers — including *you* — have been chosen and ordained by Jesus Himself to live a fruitful life. Fruitfulness will naturally result if you're doing your job as the salt of the earth. Everywhere you go will be enriched, making everything and everyone more productive.

Again, Jesus said, "…I have chosen you…" (John 15:16). The word "chosen" here is a form of the Greek word *eklegomai*, a compound of the words *ek* and *lego*. The word *ek* means *out*, and *lego* means *I say*. When these two words are joined to form *eklegomai*, it literally means, *Out, I say.*

This same word *eklegomai* is used in Ephesians 1:4, where Paul writes, "According as he hath *chosen* us in him before the foundation of the world, that we should be holy and without blame before him in love." Essentially, this means God looked out onto the vast expanse of eternity and saw each of us, and when He did, He said, "Hey, you! Out!"

What's more, the word *eklegomai* — translated here as "chosen" — means *to call out, to select, to elect,* or *to choose.* It is used to refer to *individuals who were selected for a specific purpose,* which means God has a special purpose for everyone that is called by His Name — including *you.*

The word *eklegomai* also conveys the idea of the privilege and honor of being chosen. In fact, it is so connected to the idea of privilege that those being selected should look upon themselves as honored, esteemed, and respected.

So if for any reason you are feeling condemned or not good enough, quit badgering yourself. Instead, see yourself as one that is honored, esteemed, and respected. When God looked out through the vast expanse of eternity and saw you, Jesus said, "Hey you! Out! You are the one I want."

Jesus Has 'Ordained' You To 'Bring Forth Fruit' in a Specific Place

Again, Jesus said, "Ye have not chosen me, but I have chosen you, and *ordained* you…" (John 15:16). The word "ordained" is a form of the Greek word *tithemi*, which means *to establish*, *to ordain*, or *to purposely set in place*. So once Jesus chose you by His own will, He then *established you*, *ordained you*, and *purposely set you in a specific place* "…that ye should go and bring forth fruit…" (John 15:16).

The words "bring forth" are translated from a form of the Greek word *phero*, which means *to bear* or *to carry*. It pictures something that is being carried along, like a leaf being carried by a gust of wind or like the current in a river that carries something like a fallen branch. Neither the leaf nor the branch has any inherent ability to move by itself and will only be moved if the wind or current carries it along. The same thing is true about us. Without the current of the Spirit, we are just like a powerless leaf or branch.

This word *phero* — translated here as "bring forth" — is also a technical term that was used in ancient times to denote *a ship whose sails were set to catch the wind*. The use of this word means, if we surrender to the Lord, He will empower us to do what we cannot do by ourselves. Surrendering to the Lord is how we "hoist our spiritual sails" and catch the current of the Holy Spirit. The Spirit is the One who will then carry us into a season of fruitfulness.

Always keep in mind Jesus' sobering words in John 15:5 (*NLT*):

> **…I am the vine; you are the branches. Those who remain in me, and I in them, will produce much fruit. For apart from me you can do nothing.**

If you're trying to be fruitful apart from living daily in a relationship with Jesus, you're going to be very frustrated, wear yourself out, and become exhausted. However, when you abide in fellowship with Him, you move into the current of the Holy Spirit, which is the very life of God, and He carries you into a season of fruitfulness.

Again, Jesus said that He personally chose you and ordained you, "…That ye should go and bring forth fruit…" (John 15:16). The Greek word for "fruit" here is a form of *karpos*, and it denotes *the fruit of plants or trees*. It was used to depict *the fruit borne by a person's life*, which might include *a person's deeds*, *actions*, *moral character and behavior*, or *the output of the person's work*. In essence, the word *karpos* describes the byproduct of a plant, of a tree, or of a person's life.

What this means is that if you're really abiding in the Vine — Jesus — then the sap of the Vine, which is the current of God's Spirit, will pick you up and move you into a position where you begin to bear fruit supernaturally. Remember, Jesus said, "…Apart from Me [cut off from vital union with Me] you can do nothing" (John 15:5 *AMPC*). So to produce supernatural fruit, you need to learn to live in relationship with Jesus and go with the flow of His Spirit.

The Gospel Will Produce Fruit Wherever It Goes

In Colossians 1:6, the apostle Paul said, "[The Gospel has] come unto you, as it is in all the world; and bringeth forth fruit, as it doth also in you…." The phrase "bringeth forth fruit" is translated from a form of the Greek word *karpophoreo*, and it means *to bear fruit*; *to bring forth fruit*; or *to be carried into fruitfulness*. Paul said that wherever the Gospel shows up, it brings forth fruit.

This is very important because when Jesus saved you, He also established you, gave you a purpose, and set you in place that you should bring forth much fruit. As the salt of the earth, you are like a divine fertilizer, and everywhere you go, the environment should be enriched. If you are planted where God placed you, you should expect fruitfulness.

Colossians 1:6 echoes this idea of fruitfulness. Essentially, wherever the Gospel goes, it will bring forth fruit. This truth is like a ruler you can measure your own life by to see how you're doing as the salt of the earth. If you are actively being like salt, then wherever you are the environment should be enriched, and there should be healthy, strong things being produced.

However, if you see that you have entered a season that is not producing good, healthy fruit, then something is not right. In some way, you are not doing your job as the salt of the earth. If you are being the salt of the earth, and the Gospel is going forth, you should see rich, abundant fruit. If you ever find yourself in a scenario like this, press pause on life and begin to pray, asking the Holy Spirit to show you what needs to be changed.

Friend, bearing fruit is vital. Jesus said, "By this My Father is glorified, **that you bear much fruit…**" (John 15:8 *NKJV*). You were chosen and ordained by Christ and set in place to bear fruit. As salt, you are a fertilizer, and the Gospel itself produces fruit wherever it goes. Therefore, your life should be constantly producing a bountiful harvest of good things. If it is not, you need to find out why.

'Have Salt in Yourself!'

As we wrap up this series, remember Jesus' command: "Have salt in yourselves…" (Mark 9:50). In other words, "Have all the effects and qualities for which salt is known." Here's a quick review of the seven principal uses for salt:

One: Salt was *very valuable*. As the salt of the earth, you have great value. So quit badgering yourself and putting yourself down. Instead, begin declaring, "I'm the salt of the earth, and I'm worth my salt! Jesus paid for me with His precious blood, and I carry divine treasure on the inside of me as His shaker of salt. I'm very valuable."

Two: Salt was used as *a preservative*. As salt, you ought to have a preserving effect that restrains ruin, decay, and corruption wherever you go and works jointly with the Church to restrain evil and the appearance of the antichrist.

Three: Salt was used as *a flavor enhancer*. Because you are the salt of the earth, when you show up, things should become more enjoyable and flavorful. Your presence should add spice to life and remove any blandness or monotony.

Four: Salt was used as *an antiseptic or disinfectant*, which means when you're present, contamination, sickness, and disease are dispelled and prevented from proliferating. You are God's divine antiseptic.

Five: Salt was used as *a medicinal and healing agent*. Because you are the salt of the earth, when you show up, people should get well. If they have open wounds in their body or soul (mind, emotions, or will), your presence should expedite the healing process in their life.

Six: Salt was used to provide *protection from and to drive away evil spirits*. As the salt of the earth, when you are present, you should create spiritual barriers the enemy can't breach. You and those around you will be safe because evil cannot penetrate your space. Likewise, as salt, you carry within you the delivering power of Jesus Christ, and wherever you go, you are authorized to drive out evil spirits.

Seven: Salt was used as *a fertilizer*. Because you are the salt of the earth, when you show up, the soil of your surroundings should be enriched, causing everything to become very productive.

When Jesus' hearers heard Him say, "You are the salt of the earth," they would have thought of all these things because they were the primary ways salt was used in their time. Through the power of the Holy Spirit living in you, all these aspects of salt should be active in your life.

STUDY QUESTIONS

Study to shew thyself approved unto God, a workman that needeth not to be ashamed, rightly dividing the word of truth.
— 2 Timothy 2:15

1. Jesus said He has *chosen* you, and the word *chosen* is so connected to the idea of privilege that those being selected should look upon themselves as *honored*, *esteemed*, and *respected*. Does that describe how you feel about being chosen by Jesus? If not, why? What does the enemy keep bringing back up in your mind (or what does it seem you can't forget) that is causing you to feel bad about yourself? Take time right now to pour out your heart to the Lord (*see* Psalm 62:8).

2. If you've done wrong, go to God and ask Him to forgive you of your sin. The Bible says, "If we confess our sins, he is faithful and just to forgive us our sins, and to cleanse us from all unrighteousness" (1 John 1:9). Then

ask Him for the grace to let go of the past and trust that He has forgiven you. To help you grow stronger in this godly mindset, take time to regularly reflect on and speak these promises aloud over your life:

- **God is merciful and forgiving.**
  Psalm 145:8; Isaiah 55:7; Lamentations 3:22 and 23; Micah 7:18; Titus 3:5

- **God no longer remembers my sin.**
  Psalm 103:12; Isaiah 43:25; Hebrews 8:12

- **I am not condemned or rejected.**
  John 3:17 and 18; 5:24; Romans 8:1,2,31-34

- **I am the righteousness of God in Jesus.**
  Psalm 103:17; Isaiah 61:10; Romans 8:10; 2 Corinthians 5:21

PRACTICAL APPLICATION

But be ye doers of the word, and not hearers only,
deceiving your own selves.
—James 1:22

1. Jesus has called and ordained you to produce specific, lasting **fruit** with your life. When you look back over the last year, five years, ten years, and beyond, what kind of fruit has your life produced? This would include things like your *deeds*, *actions*, *behavior*, *character*, and *accomplishments*. What fruit saddens you that you don't want to produce anymore, and what fruit are you happy and grateful for?

2. The most important thing you can set your mind and heart to learn is how to "abide in the Vine" — Christ Jesus. As you live in relationship with Him, through the Person of the Holy Spirit who is living in you, you will go with the flow of the Spirit and produce abundant, supernatural fruit. In your own words, what do you think it looks like to live in relationship with Jesus? (*Consider* Isaiah 50:4; John 14:26; 15:1-17; 16:12-15.) Knowing we always have room for improvement, what adjustments do you sense the Holy Spirit asking you to make in order to live closer to Him and be more fruitful?

---

[1] Salt statistics (https://pubs.usgs.gov/periodicals/mcs2024/mcs2024-salt.pdf, accessed 12/21/24).

Notes

Notes

Notes

A Prayer To Receive Salvation

If you've never received Jesus as your Savior and Lord, now is the time for you to experience the new life Jesus wants to give you! To receive God's gift of salvation that can be obtained through Jesus alone, pray this prayer from your heart:

Jesus, I repent of my sin and receive You as my Savior and Lord. Wash away my sin with Your precious blood and make me completely new. I thank You that my sin is removed, and Satan no longer has any right to lay claim on me. Through Your empowering grace, I faithfully promise that I will serve You as my Lord for the rest of my life.

If you just prayed this prayer of salvation, you are born again! You are a brand-new creation in Christ! Would you please let us know of your decision by going to **renner.org/salvation**? We would love to connect with you and pray for you as you begin your new life in Christ.

Scriptures for further study: John 3:16; John 14:6; Acts 4:12; Ephesians 1:7; Hebrews 10:19,20; 1 Peter 1:18,19; Romans 10:9,10; Colossians 1:13; 2 Corinthians 5:17; Romans 6:4; 1 Peter 1:3

CLAIM YOUR FREE RESOURCE!

As a way of introducing you further to the teaching ministry of Rick Renner, we would like to send you FREE of charge his teaching, "How To Receive a Miraculous Touch From God" on CD or as an MP3 download.

How To Receive
a Miraculous Touch From God
Rick Renner

CD36

R RENNER
Teaching You Can Trust

In His earthly ministry, Jesus commonly healed *all* who were sick of *all* their diseases. In this profound message, learn about the manifold dimensions of Christ's wisdom, goodness, power, and love toward all humanity who came to Him in faith with their needs.

☑ **YES, I want to receive Rick Renner's monthly teaching letter!**

Simply scan the QR code to claim this resource or go to: **renner.org/claim-your-free-offer**

Connect

WITH US!

R renner.org

f facebook.com/rickrenner • facebook.com/rennerdenise

▶ youtube.com/rennerministries • youtube.com/deniserenner

◎ instagram.com/rickrrenner • instagram.com/rennerministries_
instagram.com/rennerdenise